CONTENTS

DEDICATION

I would like to dedicate this book to my loving husband Terence and my family who provided excellent care for me when I was sick. I never would have made it without you. To all the women struggling with a life threatening disease this book is for you.

ACKNOWLEDGMENTS

To my Lord and Savior Jesus Christ who carried me through the storm, I will be forever grateful and I will share my testimony with the world about how you healed me and saved my life. I can finally say it was good that I was afflicted. You knew what was in me, and you gave me strength, protected and prepared me. You get all the glory!

To my loving husband , thank you for your consistency in prayer, for loving me through it all for showing compassion. For praying all night long to letting me just lay in your lap on Friday nights when I was too weak to go out. I am forever grateful for the fighter in you my king. For every tear you dried and all the nights you stayed up with me and for every morning you greeted me with an encouraging word about how I would make it and how you just refused to let me quit. I will love you forever.

To my amazing mom who carried me in her womb, cared for me as a child, endured my teenage years, walked me down the aisle, and taught me how to be a woman of grace and strength. I rise and call you blessed.

To my kids, Teeshlee, Cameron, Kienan and Aleece, I appreciate you all for having my back through it all, you were right there. I know it wasn't easy, but your love kept me going. To my family, my aunts and cousins I love and appreciate the ongoing support and encouragement.

To Dani, there aren't even words to say about a friend that stuck closer than a brother. Not one treatment went by without you covering me in prayer! That's love....Thank you for EVERYTHING!

To Bri, my God daughter, who knew we were connected for such a time as this... Thank you for guiding this whole book process and for showing me that sowing seeds will always produce a harvest.

To my best friend Tijuanna, to church family at Mt. Zion Church of Deliverance, Jackson and EVERYONE who prayed, fasted, visited spoke over my life, encouraged me, did my hair, cooked a meal, smiled at me, cleaned my house and ran my errands. During my darkest hours you were right there, and I love and appreciate you all.

01 The Unexpected Storm

Life has a way of breaking you down, one minute you're absolutely fine in good health and enjoying life with your family traveling taking vacations and spending time with friends when all of a sudden, a storm hits. Unexpected storms happen without any warning, it can be sunny one minute and the next minute it's raining, dark, and the winds are treacherous. An unexpected storm has the ability to destroy everything in its path in a short amount of time. During an unexpected storm you don't have time to run for cover. During this unpredictable weather darkness covers the sky and hail falls and even trees with deep roots are often uprooted and blow over. This is exactly how I felt when the doctor said to me, It's Cancer! My unexpected storm caused darkness to invade my life, for me to feel blown over, feeling as if I had no time to take cover. I felt hopeless and lost but only for a moment.

The unexpected storms we face in life often take our breath away. It's as if all we have been taught is put to the test, all at once. No one in my family had ever faced cancer but they had experienced other types of unexpected storms. I can recall the battles they faced and through every heartache, sickness, death, and disappointment they always leaned on God. I come from a strong family of faith, who believes that God can do anything. They taught me that prayer and fasting would always work. It seemed to make their loads lighter. To be honest I had been praying and seeking God and I felt that my faith was stronger than ever... until the storm came. For a moment I was stunned, discouraged, and even fearful but I turned to the only thing that has ever worked and that was my Faith in God. Though the storm was unexpected I knew that God would not leave me and allow me to drown. I began to reflect on Gods greatness and though it looked hopeless, and I felt lost, I turned to the only think I know and held on to Gods promises and Gods word began to minister to me. Its as if his words penetrated the darkness that I was facing.

The Lord himself goes before you and will be with you; he will never leave you nor forsake you. Do not be afraid; do not be discouraged" (Deuteronomy 31:8 *NIV*).

I must admit at times I was very afraid; I wept and I had many sleepless nights. I knew that it was ok to experience moments of fear and I was even reminded it was normal, but it wasn't real. I once heard a preacher say that fear is just perverted faith. Fear is one of the enemy's biggest weapons formed to keep us blinded from the promises of God. When we embrace the spirit of fear, we forget about Gods word. The enemy tricks us into thinking that God has abandoned us. He constantly feeds us lies about our future and if we are not careful his lies will ultimately captivate and control all of our thoughts. "For God hath not given us the spirit of fear; but of power, and of love and of a sound mind" (2 Timothy 1:7 *KJV*).

I was led to consider Peter who followed Jesus closely and witnessed many miracles, yet he experienced fear. Jesus kindly said: "Stop being afraid. From now on you will be catching men alive." (Luke 5:10, 11) This was no time for doubt or fear. Peter later became a bold man and even walked on water but time after time his doubts and fears kept him from being man of strength. The man who called himself "a witness of the sufferings of Christ" (1 Peter 5:1) was not there when Jesus was hanging on the cross; he was hiding in fear. The man who calls us to be eager to serve (1 Peter 5:2) remained seated while Jesus washed the disciples' feet.

The man who tells us that we should be clear-minded and self-controlled so that we can pray (1 Peter 4:7) fell asleep while Jesus was sweating blood. The man who so boldly tells us, "Submit yourselves for the Lord's sake to every human authority" (1 Peter 2:13 *NIV*) cut off the soldier Malchus's ear in the garden (John 18:10–11). He had moments of bravery but often allowed fear to control him.

No matter what type of unexpected storm you are facing you must realize this is no time to fear. Instead of embracing your fears, become fixated on your faith.

Speak the word over fear:

Isaiah 41:10 "So do not fear, for I am with you; do not be dismayed, for I am your God. I will strengthen you and help you; I will uphold you with my righteous right hand."

Psalm 56:3 "When I am afraid, I put my trust in you."

Philippians 4:6-7 "Do not be anxious about anything, but in every situation, by prayer and petition, with thanksgiving, present your requests to God. And the peace of God, which transcends all understanding, will guard your hearts and your minds in Christ Jesus."

John 14:27 "Peace is what I leave with you; it is my own peace that I give you. I do not give it as the world does. Do not be worried and upset; do not be afraid."

2 Timothy 1:7 "For God has not given us a spirit of fear, but of power and of love and of a sound mind."

1 John 4:18 "There is no fear in love. But perfect love drives out fear, because fear has to do with punishment. The one who fears is not made perfect in love."

Psalm 94:19 "When anxiety was great within me, your consolation brought joy to my soul."

Isaiah 43:1 "But now, this is what the Lord says…Fear not, for I have redeemed you; I have summoned you by name; you are mine."

Proverbs 12:25 "An anxious heart weighs a man down, but a kind word cheers him up."

Psalm 23:4 "Even though I walk through the valley of the shadow of death, I will fear no evil, for you are with me; your rod and your staff, they comfort me."

Joshua 1:9 "Have I not commanded you? Be strong and courageous. Do not be terrified; do not be discouraged, for the Lord your God will be with you wherever you go."

Prayer

Dear Heavenly Father I know that you are with me even through the unexpected storms. Please wrap your arms around me during my times of fear and deliver me from worry and anxiety. Help me to trust you more day by day.
Amen.

Journal

Reflect on the trials that you are facing and what causes you fear. Decree and declare that you will no longer live in fear and that you choose a life of faith.

_____

_____

_____

_____

_____

_____

_____

_____

_____

_____

_____
_____
_____
_____
_____
_____
_____
_____
_____
_____
_____
_____
_____
_____
_____
_____
_____
_____
_____
_____
_____
_____
_____
_____
_____
_____
_____
_____

02 I See Victory

I am excited to have the opportunity to share my story for His glory. After being told that I had cancer, my heart sank and I felt lost and confused. If I can bear my heart for a moment, I felt surprised that I had been hit with such horrible news. I thought that because I was a born again Christian and we had no family who had ever been diagnosed with cancer that it must be a mistake. Why would God allow me to face this giant at this point in my life. Who would I turn to, and what did I do to deserve this were the questions I had. I had no point of reference on how to defeat this giant. When you are hit with an unforeseen storm in your life you have got to step back and make a faith confession that will cause the enemy to start shaking in his boots. Even if the enemy throws something big at you, and you feel shaken, don't lose it! It may hit you but declare it won't kill you. Don't allow your storms to bury you, allow them to build you. You have to declare victory at the beginning of the storm. So when my doctor said I'm sorry Mrs. Hawkins, its cancer, I declared I don't receive that into my spirit....I shall live and declare the works of the Lord. She said well if you don't receive it, I guess you will be my walking miracle. I used my faith confession to change the direction of the entire situation from the beginning.

You must watch what you allow to come out of your mouth. The word says that death and life are in the power of your tongue. What you speak you shall receive. I chose in that moment to speak life. It did not look good but I'm so grateful that we walk by faith and not by sight. You have got to get a vision in your mind of you being healed, so that when the doctor says you are sick, you declare you are healed, when turmoil hits your home you can declare we are more than conquerors through Christ. You have to take on the mindset that no matter what comes or goes I am destined to be a winner. Just cry out now as you continue to read. I must win!

I had been a fairly healthy person, I ate a few too many pieces of chicken from time to time but overall I was healthy and had never been afflicted with any life altering illness. In a moment it appeared that out of nowhere my life changed. I didn't have time to wonder what to do next, I had to work with what I had been given which was power over the enemy and I had to immediately reject the voice of the enemy. When the enemy spoke death I declared "I do not receive it" and I held on to my faith. In your season of turmoil you have got to hold on to your faith. You have to immediately silence the voice of the enemy with your praise, your worship and your faith confessions.

To make a very long story short in 2018 I was diagnosed with cancer, I had to endure a year and half worth of chemotherapy and about 56 radiation treatments. During this time I sustained second and third degree burns, experienced weakness and sickness like nothing I had ever felt. When initially diagnosed, I said I'll be strong, I won't lose my hair, I won't handle this situation like everyone else, because I am called and anointed. I said I would not need chemo or radiation. Basically, I was telling God how I wanted the process to work and how I wanted the storm to be structured. God had other plans! I lost all of my hair, all of my eye lashes and eyebrows. Due to the medication all of my fingernails and toenails turned black, even my tongue turned black. I experienced extreme joint pain, mouth sores, skin irritations, weakened eye sight, insomnia, memory loss, swelling and a number of other side effects related to the medication.

When you are going through a storm, you must understand that God has a plan. Through all the physical issues and pain, I knew God was in control. At times it felt that He was so far away, and that He wasn't answering my prayers, but I had to remind myself that he allows us to go through things to make us strong. My prognosis was not favorable and required that I endure a lot of pain. I didn't get angry with God, I just utilized those moments to give God more glory. Each time I went to chemotherapy I would find someone to share the love of Christ with. In the darkest hour of your life you have to be determined to be a light and to continuously declare victory.

There were times I wasn't feeling optimistic and the pain made it hard to even smile, but I continued to declare victory. This was a very painful time in my life but I refused to give up. I don't want it to seem like I just floated through the storm and never doubted, because that's very inaccurate, I stumbled, kicked and cried, but I refused to stay in a low place. On occasion my faith would waiver, but I refused to stay in that place. When you find yourself in a low place you have got to find a scripture and a song to meditate on and hold on. Just find enough strength to say…"My only hope is his only son Jesus". When you can't say anything else, just call on the name of Jesus. The situation doesn't always change immediately but you begin to change. Your perception changes, your pain decreases, and your endurance increases when you just call the name of Jesus.

Many days I would cry out and say God if you don't help me, I don't know what I will do. I pleaded with God to get me out of the storm, and he kindly replied the only way out is through…. Meaning I had to complete the process. It wasn't until the end of the storm that I realized that God was making me in the process. There are some storms you don't get to pass through quickly you have got to stay there and complete the process. It was not easy, but I knew that enduring the storm would make me stronger! I knew it was a part of my destiny, and that I would have a testimony. I was on a rocky road to victory, but it was worth it. I knew the enemy wanted to destroy my life, but God promised that if I went through the process that I would come out with victory. I held on through the pain and through the storm and came out with total victory.

Even when you don't see the victory, you can stand on the promises of God, and declare the word of Lord. Know that He is with you and that even in your darkest season you will receive victory. You are not alone! I want to encourage you that victory is coming. It may not feel like it, it may not look like it, everyone around you even the doctors may be skeptical. Exercise your God given right and declare the word over your life and say I declare VICTORY!

Speak the word over your situation:

Deuteronomy 20:4 "For the LORD your God is the one who goes with you to fight for you against your enemies to give you victory."

John 16:33 "I have told you these things, so that in me you may have peace. In this world you will have trouble. But take heart! I have overcome the world."

Ephesians 6:13 "Therefore put on the full armor of God, so that when the day of evil comes, you may be able to stand your ground, and after you have done everything, to stand."

1 Corinthians 9:24 "Do you not know that those who run in a race all run, but only one receives the prize? Run in such a way that you may win."

Prayer

Dear heavenly father, we thank you because your word says that we are more than conquerors through Jesus Christ. We thank you that the weapons formed cannot prosper. We thank you because what the enemy meant for evil, you turned it around for my good. Thank you father that we realize that trouble won't last always and this too shall pass. Weeping may endure but for a night and I believe and decree that my morning season is coming. Thank you for the victory to overcome every situation and challenge that life may bring. Please help us to realize that if we go through, that victory is waiting for us on the other side. In the mighty name of Jesus. Amen

Journal

List all the areas in your life that you need God to help you obtain victory and speak to those situations. Begin to speak victory over those situations in your life daily. As you obtain victory in the areas you are journaling about cross them off the list and give God glory for the victory.

_____

_____

_____

_____

_____

_____

_____

_____

_____

_____

_____

_____

_____

_____

_____

_____

_____

_____

_____

_____

_____

_____

03 I Know it's Raining...
But Keep Standing

I can recall walking into radiation totally exhausted, in extreme pain, burned and bloody. I prayed all the way to radiation hoping that they would say I didn't need more treatment, but that was not the case. They stated I needed to finish ALL of my treatments. I was discouraged, and feelings of defeat flooded my soul... but I heard my husband say "through every storm and every trial it's important to finish strong." So with tears running down my face I walked in for another treatment.

In this life you are going to face a many storms, and it may be raining really hard in your life right now, but I want to encourage you to keep standing. I know you been going through a lot of rough stuff, and it feels like you've been set up to fail. Everything you have set out to do to fix your situation has not worked. But be encouraged, because you are being set up to win. Have faith in God, not in yourself. Trust in the Lord and lean not to your own understanding. When it's raining in your life, you have to know that God is with you and He will bring you through. Don't let your storm sweep you away, hold on! If you can stand in the rain get ready because you are about to experience another dimension of His glory.

Discouragement is designed to deter our destiny, and diminish our dreams. There are tough issues we face and situations that can only be changed by the hand of God. If you can stand the rain and keep exercising your faith and focus on finishing strong. You will experience another dimension of His glory and will be positioned to receive blessings and miracles. You must pray in faith. Therefore I say unto you, What things soever ye desire, when ye pray, believe that ye receive *them*, and ye shall have *them* (Mark 11:24). When you pray and study the word, it will produce faith. Your situation says you won't survive but your faith rises up and says the favor of God is on me. Yes it's raining in my life but I still have favor and I'll make it through this storm. When you believe in Gods promises you can stand the rain.

Every area may feel like it is under attack but don't get distracted by the rain and forget that on the other side of that trial is your testimony. I know you have been hurt and yes, you've been beat up, but keep standing because your breakthrough is coming. Yes, it's been raining in your life, and the divorce hurt, and the kids are still acting up, the doctor said there is nothing else they can do and your job is unfulfilling. Just keep on standing in the rain and declaring the word. You will not only survive it but you will thrive and recover all that you lost in your rainy season. The word say's many are the afflictions of the righteous but the Lord delivereth him out of them all (Psalm 34:19). The good news is that, we have a comforter. Even though it may be raining right now in your life, the Lord is going to deliver us out of all of our trouble. There is nothing too great or too small for our God.

It is written in the word, we are going to face some trials and trouble (Job 14:1) BUT that's not the end of the story. Don't quit in the middle of the storm, get to the end and fulfill your purpose in life. So know this, that in the fight he's going with you; "For the LORD your God is he that goeth with you, to fight for you against your enemies, to save you" (Deuteronomy 20:4). But you got to get back up after a fall and be determined to win. When you feel too weak to fight, you have to meditate on the scripture over and over.

"I can do all things through Christ which strengthen me (Philippians 4:13). The enemy is constantly telling you, you will never make it you can't do this and you aren't strong enough. That is a lie! YOU HAVE GOT TO BELIEVE THE WORD OF GOD. You will WIN!

Realize that you are being made! Yes, I know it's raining now but keep standing. You are being made into something amazing. I started to think about how fine wine is made. First the grapes are handpicked and then cleaned. After the cleansing the grapes are crushed. Hot water is then poured over the crushed grapes to make sure nothing is left that may change the flavor. Then its left to sit for a while and ferment. During the fermenting stage it appears to be just sitting there but something is happening whether it looks like it or not. One of the most important parts of the fermentation process is that during this process the wine must be covered; there are things happening that you can't see. Then after the process is complete, you have fine wine. Let me tell you, you are in the process. You might not see it happening but you are being covered in the process!!! You are being made into something fine. It feels like God has just left you there to sit for a while all alone and that nothing is happening. But God is working on your behalf. If you can just hold on and stand the rain and go through the process, you will walk right into your "YES" season.

Let's look at Noah and what happened when he was asked can you stand the rain?

<u>Scripture Genesis 7 1:5</u>

The LORD then said to Noah, "Go into the ark, you and your whole family, because I have found you righteous in this generation. **2** Take with you seven pairs of every kind of clean animal, a male and its mate, and one pair of every kind of unclean animal, a male and its mate, **3** and also seven pairs of every kind of bird, male and female, to keep their various kinds alive throughout the earth. **4** Seven days from now I will send rain on the earth for forty days and forty nights, and I will wipe from the face of the earth every living creature I have made." **5** And Noah did all that the LORD commanded him.

1. God to Noah build an Ark because it's going to rain.
2. People laughed at him and thought he was crazy because it hadn't rained
3. He followed Gods instruction and built an Ark.
4. He got in the ark before it actually started raining (rained 7 days later)
5. Sure enough it started raining and raining enough to flood the whole earth. The flood was massive. It rained for 40 days and 40 nights but the flood lasted for 150 days! They stayed in the ark with those animals until God said get out.

As a result of Noah trusting the plan of God, he and his family were saved from the flood. You have got to trust the plan. All those people that laughed at Noah, couldn't stand the rain. All the people who didn't trust Gods plan couldn't stand the rain. All the people in your life laughing at you when you follow the plan of God, will eventually be swept away by their own storms. So just be determined that even though it's raining you will follow and trust Gods plan.

Noah heard the plan and started building. You got to start building. Building what? Your prayer life, your faith, your spiritual stamina! Some of your prayer lives need a renovation. Operation total make over needs to occur. Often times we only pray when there's a crisis or an emergency. but it's time to pray without ceasing. Pray before it starts raining so if its sprinkling or it's a storm you can stand the rain. You have got to prepare for what's coming! You have got to be like Noah he wasn't worried about the rain because he was prepared. He knew that when the rain stopped he would see the victory. It's not going to rain forever in your life. Sooner than you think the rain is going to stop!

So when the storms rage in your life, you can be confident and know that you are being set up for greater, you are being led to a place of victory, and after you have suffered a while you will come out stronger. Be encouraged that If God brought you to it, he's got to bring you through it. Continue to be faithful and obey and God will help you stand through every storm.

Prayer

Father in the name of Jesus I thank you that I am totally equipped for the storm. I know that you are with me and I am ready for what is coming my way, and even though it's raining really hard right now, I believe that you are with me in the storm. In my weakness you are made strong. I am grateful for the storm winds that blew my way but they did not take me out. Though I was battered by the storm, your grace and mercy covered me. I know your grace and mercy will sustain me and for that I am grateful. Continue to guide me through life's stormy season. In Jesus Name Amen.

Scripture

1 Peter 5:10 "But the God of all grace, who hath called us unto his eternal glory by Christ Jesus, after that ye have suffered a while, make you perfect, stablish, strengthen, settle you."

Journal

List all the areas in your life that you need to rebuild: your prayer life, your alone time with God, your faith, etc. List specific daily actions you will take to change the outcome of your storm. What do you need to implement to assure a strong finish?

_____

_____

_____

_____

_____

_____

_____

_____

_____

_____

_____

17

04 It Will Birth Purpose

There are times when I look back on the pain that cancer caused and wonder why would a loving God put me through so much pain. I was instantly checked in my spirit, God did not put you through pain, to break you, He didn't cause sickness to come upon you to kill you. He allowed it to happen and he knew it was necessary for you to go through it so you could reach your destiny. You may be thinking the same thing. Why did my husband leave me, why are my kids acting out, why am I broke, will I ever be promoted, will people always betray me? The trial and storm you are going through that seems to be never ending, has a purpose. Your pain has a purpose. You must realize there's a blessing in your brokenness. When you face the worse season of your life you have to approach it realizing that it has a purpose.

Meditate on God's Word

There are a few things you must do while going through the storm. One of the most important things is to meditate on God's word. Read it, and quote it over and over. You might have heard that meditating on God's word will bring you peace. I knew how to pray, I knew how to fast, but I didn't know what it meant to meditate on God's word. Meditate is defined as to **sit quietly and clear the mind or be deep in thought**. When you are in your storm you need to sit quietly, and clear your mind, and focus on the spirit of God. When you have a clear mind you can focus on what God is saying. When I was going through chemo I would play the word of God in my earbuds on a regular basis. My husband made a CD full of healing scriptures and we played them in our home often during the day and night. In the middle of the storm I would have awful nightmares; I would dream I was going to die, and I would see myself in a casket, with my family crying all around me. I would wake up shaking and sweating. My husband would rock me and say it was only a dream, you are covered by the blood of Jesus. He would say roll over let me hold you and would pray in my ear until I fell back to sleep. Playing the healing scriptures at night helped me sleep peacefully through the night and deterred night terrors.

Speak God's Word

You have to put the word on your situation and speak it every day! Wake up and declare the word, all day long, speaking the word over your situation until it changes. I had healing scriptures and declarations in my daughter Aleece's bathroom, which stated "my mom is strong and totally healed." When faced with the battle of cancer you must realize that the enemy wants to torment you and everyone attached to you. Not only was it important for me to confess the word and positive life giving declarations, it was important for my entire family to gain strength through their confessions as well.

My daughter was 12 when this all started and it was very frightening for her. I can recall the tears rolling down her face as she asked "mom are you going to die?" it broke my heart that she had to carry such a burden. I then knew the enemy was out to destroy my whole family, and tried to load us with the spirit of fear. I told her to quote "God has not given us the spirit of fear" every day. I assured her, I would not die until God said it was my time, and that I am a warrior, built to last. I told her I wanted to see her graduate and marry a nice young man. I wasn't going to allow the enemy to take me out and steal those opportunities from me. It helped shape her prayer life at an early age. There are scriptures still posted all over our home. On our back door I posted so she could see it as she left the house... "my mommy is healed and my mommy is a warrior." She read it so much that it settled her spirit and day by day she started to believe I would live and her smile came back.

You must get in the practice of confessing the promises of God. What is the Lord saying about you? You must read the word and speak the word of God. There is power in your words! You have to put the word on your situation and speak it every day! Wake up and declare the word, all day speak the word over your situation. God's word will transform your life. Tap into the power of God's word! Make a habit of speaking Gods word over your situation that concerns you daily, and it MUST change. When you practice saying what God says about you, you will live the life God wants you to live. When I was going through my storm I had to confess daily that I am already healed.

Proverb 18:21 "Death and life are in the power of the tongue: and they that love it shall eat the fruit thereof "

Philippians 4:13 "I can do all things through Christ which strengtheneth me."

Jeremiah 17:14 "Heal me, O Lord, and I shall be healed: save me, and I shall be saved: for thou art my praise"

Hebrews 4:12 "For the word of God [is] quick, and powerful, and sharper than any two edged sword, piercing even to the dividing asunder of soul and spirit, and of the joints and marrow, and [is] a discerner of the thoughts and intents of the heart."

Praying
You must Pray. Plain and simple, you must make time for prayer. The key to defeating whatever attack the enemy launches

21

on you is prayer. *Prayer is the key to your spiritual success.* When you spend time talking to God and listening to his answer you will be able to face your storm with the right posture. Prayer is a solemn request for help! Prayer gives you strength, prayer gives you power over the enemy. Prayer makes you focus on the solution as opposed to the storm. Prayer, ushers you into the presence of God. Prayer is a time when you can give God thanks for sustaining you and for blessing you. Therefore I say unto you, What things soever ye desire, when ye pray, believe that ye receive them, and ye shall have them (Mark 11:24).

When I was in chemotherapy and undergoing radiation it was painful. My physical body was in extreme pain. I had never felt so defeated in my life. As I previously stated, my mind was clouded and I had to fight the spirit of fear daily. Physically everything about me was changing; by this time I was gaining weight, and I had lost all the hair on my body. I was completely bald and I didn't feel attractive at all. I felt somewhat insecure and at times unstable. I had to wear wigs and needed to buy bigger clothing but I had no energy to shop. The enemy was speaking as loud as he could in my ear and would tell me each day, you are going to die! He would speak to me and say things like… "You will not see your daughter graduate or get married. Your husband will be a widower and your other kids will die of a broken heart when you leave them. You won't get to see your grandkids grow up." I had days where I barely left my bedroom and the spirit of depression would come knocking on my door when I spent time alone. I would get anxious, especially when I was home alone, because I knew I would have to spend significant time fighting the devil.

I thank God that I was taught the word of God and I trusted every promise it said about me. Every day I talked back to the enemy. I shall live and not die and declare the works of the Lord. I know that the word says that by His stripes I am healed. I knew His word said I am the head and not the tail. I knew the word said I had the power to speak to my mountain and it would throw itself into the sea. I knew and declared that no weapon formed against me shall prosper! I played the word of God in my house loudly for hours early in the morning and sometimes late at night. My husband would roll over and ask if I was awake and he would just begin to speak and pray the word in my ear. I thank God for an amazing supportive man of God in my life. Everyone needs a person that will get in the fight with them. My husband was in the fight with me, when I would be too exhausted to go on, he would be right there praying and fighting, and pushing me to get up and keep going. I pray you find that special someone who will stand with you and support you. So if its cancer you are facing, if its diabetes, a brain tumor, or any life threatening disease. You must make up in your mind that God is in control and no matter what the diagnosis, you will FIGHT in the spirit until your very last breath. You must use your spiritual weapons! Knowing that in the end you expect to WIN!

When you are facing a battle, you must hold on to the tools above. Though I was physically sick and under attack from the enemy I never stopped praying, I continued to worship and praise. You must push past how you feel physically and allow your sprit man to do all the work. Even if you can't walk, you can still pray. If you can't get off the couch, you can still read the word. I fed myself a daily diet of the word and each day I got spiritually stronger. After I gained spiritual strength the body lined up and I got physically stronger as well. The word strengthened me, the word healed me and the word kept me. It was painful but it was worth it. It helped me to birth my purpose. When the trial gets hot and heavy you must decree, it's not going to kill me, it's going to push me closer to my purpose. Don't allow this storm to kill you. Your storm must produce fruit. You must know you are going to come out with more! Do not die in the storm! You must LIVE!

Daily Scriptures to confess over your situation:

Romans 6:11 "I am dead to sin and alive unto righteousness."

2 Corinthians 5:17 "I am a new creature in Christ: old things have passed away, behold, all things are new."

Isaiah 54:17 "No weapon that is formed against me shall prosper, but every tongue that rises against me in judgment, I shall show to be in the wrong."

Jeremiah 29:11 "I prosper in everything I put my hand to. I have prosperity in all areas of my life—spiritually, financially, mentally, and socially."

2 Corinthians 10:5 "I take every thought captive unto the obedience of Jesus Christ, casting down every imagination, and every high and lofty thing that exalts itself against the knowledge of God."
James 1:19 "I am slow to speak, quick to hear, and slow to anger."

James 1:22; Psalm 1:2 "I am a doer of the Word. I meditate on the Word all the day long."
2 Timothy 2:15; Luke 18:1 "I will study the Word of God. I will pray."

Prayer

Father in the name of Jesus, I pray that the readers will grow in strength, that they will desire more of you. That through daily reading and confessing your word, that we will become stronger. Your word is true and we declare that we have victory. We declare that the weapons formed against us will not prosper. Lord help us to hold on, and even in our most painful moment, we declare that we shall win. I pray that you give us an anointing to face our battles and that each trial make us stronger.

Journal
Write down your purpose and the steps you will take to live out your God given destiny.

_____

_____

_____

_____

_____

_____

_____

_____
_____
_____
_____
_____
_____
_____
_____
_____
_____
_____
_____
_____
_____
_____
_____
_____
_____
_____
_____
_____
_____
_____
_____
_____

05 Talking to Mountains

Matthew 17: 20 "If you have faith, the size of a mustard seed, you can say to the mountain, remove hence to yonder place - and it shall remove. And nothing shall be impossible for you."

Matthew 21:21 "If you believe Gods word you can tell mountains to throw themselves into the sea and it will be done."

When I was young my grandmother used to say things like, "you better talk to that mountain and tell it to move." I didn't have a clue what she was trying to tell me. She used parables and scriptures I didn't understand. Speaking to a mountain didn't really mean anything to me until much later in life. The Bible says that if you have faith, which is simply belief in God's word, I could talk to my problems and they would have to leave me. Actually, the Bible says it like this: "if you have the faith and believe, you can say to a mountain – Get out of my way! And it must move. Still the phrase wasn't clear to me until mountains started getting in my way. It wasn't until I had a huge mountain right in front of me and had tried everything on my own to move it, that I realized what that scripture meant.

So, what do mountains symbolize in today's society? Mountains represent debt, the job you hate, the job you can't find, rebellious kids, baby mama drama, unforgiveness of self, defeat, low self-esteem and faithlessness. So many mountains appear in our lives as foreclosed homes and drug addictions. Some look like pornography and sexual immorality. Some mountains look like family conflict. There is a mountain that looks like depression and one that looks like suicide. There are also huge mountains that look like hopelessness and failure. Denali is the highest mountain peak in the U.S and North America, and represents, the impossible. Many have tried to conquer its peaks, and many have failed. Now that I've faced my own mountains, I know just what mountains look like, because I have faced many of them. Cancer was the mountain that I had to face and defeat. And I did!

We all have mountains to face, but we must believe that once you give your life to God, you never have to face another mountain alone. The Lord says I love you, more than you love you. What you need to do when you're facing a mountain is to give God praise. If you have faith and do not doubt, you can say to the mountain, go throw yourself into the sea, and it will be done. What the sea represents is a place that is so deep that things that are cast into it, can never be recovered. It's gone forever.

So, put on your spiritual game face, your armour, your fatigues, and speak to the mountains in your life. You're going to need the confidence of a warrior, the spirit of a warrior, the strength of a warrior and the tenacity of a warrior. Don't let the enemy scare you into backing down. No weapon formed against you can prosper. The enemy uses a number of scare tactics because he knows the power that God put in you.

Get to the point where you can have peace, where you can be alone and not feel lonely, where you can start trusting again, where you can forgive others, where you can feel good about who you are and what you are doing. Get to a place where you don't have to ask yourself "is this mountain going to destroy me"? Or am I going to destroy it? Be a giant slayer like David and speak to your mountain and tell it, like my gramma told me to say to my mountains, Move mountain! It's time to fight and WIN! It's time to release the warrior in you!

06 Burned, But Still Standing

Isaiah 43:2 "When I walk through the fire and the flood I will not be consumed because the Lord is with me."

Ephesians 6:13-14 "Therefore take up the whole armor of God, that you may be able to stand in the evil day, and having done all, to stand."

I was watching the news the other day and the weatherman was showing a clip of a forest fire. He was pointing out the devastation and how many homes were lost. He said it sometimes takes several months to build a new home. Most of the foliage and trees were obliterated. He stated that it is possible for much of the foliage to grow back and flourish again. Unfortunately, it takes many years for trees to grow back. Some trees were young, and some were old. Some had been in that forest, for over sixty years and had very deep roots. Many were over fifty feet tall.

The reporter mentioned the different types of trees that were damaged. Several different species were in that forest and started as seedlings. As he was talking, the camera man was capturing the destruction. Then the reporter said, "what you are seeing now, are burned trees that are still standing". I remember vividly, dropping what I had in my hand in disbelief. I had never imagined that a tree that was charred as black as coal, with no branches left, no leaves and no bark, could still be standing. I said to myself, God! That is what some Christians are going through right now. Burned but still standing. Many Christians are going through fiery trials, but they are also coming out. They have been devastated by fiery situations, but they didn't succumb to the flames. Some feel like they are living in a burned house right now. Some have visited people whose homes have been devastated by fire. It's very sad to view. There's nothing left. No walls, no roof, no floors, no photos, no heirlooms, no furniture. Nothing.

We that have been through devastation, know how important it is to keep standing after you've been deeply hurt spiritually. Sometimes it's our family or our closest friend that hurts us. That makes us feel like we have been in a fire. What we thought we had; we no longer have. In an instant, everything is gone. No closeness, no love, no commitment.

Experts say that some burned trees are still useful. They still have value. They can still become a treasure to someone. What happens is that the inside is still good and usable. A master craftsman carves the burned surface away and what is left is a fine piece of cured wood. Cured wood is used to make some of the most beautiful, sturdy, everlasting pieces of artwork, ever seen. Some trees become bannisters, columns, and canes. All of which are used to support others. So, after they have already been through the fire, they would not be expected to hold up or support anything else. We need to know that God is the Master craftsman that we need. God needs a burned tree. God wants a burned tree. God is looking for a burned tree. Because we have been burned but still standing, God needs you to know that you are more valuable than the tree that is now ash on the forest floor. You are more valuable than the tree that was knocked down by another tree, and of course, couldn't get out from under it. You are more valuable to the people that are living in a house, with you as their door. Be proud of your ability to be a protector of others. Protect those that have been burned as you once were. Let them know how valuable they are.

Fiery trials can burn us. The cancer diagnosis burned me, but I'm still standing. They can leave us feeling charred, uprooted, broken, barren and useless. But although you have been burned, keep standing, keep growing, keep swaying, but don't ever break. You are not ash, you are not useless, you are not hopeless. You are the tree that God spoke of in the Bible. You are a tree of Righteousness. Now grow, flourish, and reach for the sky. After you have done all you can to stand…keep standing!

Dear warrior, after all you have gone through you are still standing. I want to let you know that God is never going to leave you nor forsake you, he promised that in His word. Don't fear, is in the Bible 365 times! The Father wants us to be sure we have a clear understanding that we have no reason to fear. The Lord is with you during your hardest times and your darkest hours. Be determined to fight and know that you are destined to win. Remember that trouble don't last always, and weeping may endure but for a night but joy is coming… I call forth the warrior in you! Now stand up and FIGHT!

PART II
Daily
Devotions for
the Warrior in
You

By Charisse Chatman

When I Wake

Lord, when I wake, I want joy to pull me out of bed in the morning. Passion for the word to guide me to the shower. The anointing to sit at the breakfast table with me as I read my devotion, praise to embrace me as I seek Your face, and Your glory to surround me, as I leave my home.

In My Room
When I woke up this morning the SUN was peeking through my window. And when I got up the spirit of the SON was in my room.

I Remember When

I can remember looking out the window in the middle of the night and being amazed by what appeared to be diamond dust, covering the fresh fallen snow in my back yard. It was beautiful. Only God could create such a scenic, real life portrait.

I remember asking the Lord, why is it that I see such beautiful things when I am all alone. Before I could finish my thought, the Holy Spirit said, "you have never been alone." Not one time did I allow you to see the works of My hands alone. I have been with you for every rainbow, every waterfall, every mountain top, every ocean sunrise, every multicolored sunset, every hummingbird, flowers that have pushed their way through the asphalt, a full moon, and amazing cloud formations. All these things I have given you and I have been with you when you first saw them and recognized My power. I have never left you and will never leave you. I delight in you, for delighting in Me, and what My hands have created.

Take a moment and reflect on Gods presence. You can be at peace because God is right there with you. He will not leave you alone.

Rain on Me

Matthew 5:45 "The Lord rains on the just as well as the unjust."

A lot of sinners will be blessed this year, and some believers will be mad about it. If we are to do the opposite of whatever the world does, then instead of running to get out of the rain, we should be running to get in the rain (spiritually). When we are unsaved, and it rains we just get wet. But when we are saved and it rains, we get what the rain produces! We get soaked in the anointing, drenched with joy, covered like an umbrella, with peace. People search us out. They want our advice; they want the presence of God that they see in us and on us. We hold in our root's life-giving sustenance for the times when we face inevitable droughts.

Being in the presence of the Holy Spirit is the closest thing to reliving your innocent childhood. Remember when you were standing in the rain with arms outstretched and your face turned toward heaven? You were expecting rain to fall on your tongue, in anticipation of a mouthful of raindrops. It didn't happen, but every drop that you did feel made you smile in anticipation of the next. That's how the Holy Spirit makes us feel!

There will be a lot of trials this year, so... like there is every year. But, be encouraged. God is not dead. He is waiting and planning to take us through the things that have not happened yet. Some of us will face sickness, disease, and death. Some families will face divorce, breakups, and rebellious children. This week I thanked God for taking me through last year but now I need to thank him for taking me through this year so far.

Every day we face a possible trial or triumph. Tragedy and trials are inevitable in this fallen world. But the assurance that we have is that we never have to face anything alone. The Lord has promised to be with us always. Now what I do every day is to thank him for every smile, and every tear, for every laugh and every moan. For every good day and every bad. For every sunshiny day and every storm, for every wedding and every funeral. I know that in all situations to give thanks. I thank Him for every compliment but much more the insults I endured, because they made me stronger.

Lord rain on me. Everyday.

I Can't See the Ram

Gen 22:9-13 "A ram in the bush"

Isaiah 41:10 "I will uphold you with my righteous right hand"

The Ram in the bush is a well-known story in the Bible. Abraham was told by God to sacrifice his son Isaac. At the last-minute God provided a ram in the bush, which allowed Abraham to spare his sons life.

Sometimes we don't know what we should do in certain situations. We do, however, know that your word says, "I will always provide a way of escape for you." When we are in a life changing situation, all we know is that we feel paralyzed with fear. But if we are children of God, adopted into His family, obeying His commands and keep His statutes, He will always provide a way of escape for us.

We have all had times when we thought we were doing exactly what we were supposed to do, and even more. We cry out saying "God, I'm obeying your commands, I'm doing what you told me to do. I'm witnessing, praying, fasting, giving, lamenting, encouraging, studying your word, honoring, and much more". I believe if I obey your word, I will eventually see what you have for me. You are waiting for me to act, the way you waited to see if Abraham was going to sacrifice his son. Will I obey you? Will I trust you? Will I believe you? I know the next move is mine.

I believe if I obey…We think surely, God will step in at the last minute, and we'll hear, something happened at the office and I did get the position. We thought the doctor was going to say that the tests were wrong, we don't have cancer. We thought our finances would be straightened out, without having to sell our home.

But what if you wait on God and still don't see the ram? You sacrificed your last offering in church, and you expected it back, and now you aren't sure what is going to happen with your bills. What if you sacrificed your sleep and stayed up all night petitioning God about our child, and they still went to prison. What if you sacrificed everything, and now you have nothing? What if you don't see the ram? What if everything in my life looks like muddy water and feels like thorns piercing my flesh. What if all I see is darkness an all I feel is heartache. What if my dreams are all nightmares and my straight places are all crooked? What if that sweet smell of flowers smells putrid to me. What if my sun never shine, and my nights have no stars? What if my life is no longer worth living?

God! What if I can't see the Ram! I have no choice but to put all my trust in You Lord. I will believe only in you. I praise only You. I follow only You. I worship only You. Show me the ram that You have waiting for me Lord. Show me.

From The Desert To The River

Exodus 23:20-31 "I will send an angel before you."

2 Kings 3:18 "This is an easy thing in the eyes of the Lord."

Isaiah 54:17 "No Weapon formed against you will prosper."

As I sit here with six dollars in my checking account, reading a passage of scripture that came to me regarding Gods blessings, I decided to encourage myself through His word. "No weapon formed against me shall prosper. "

The Lord was going to grant the Israelites a huge portion of land, from the Red Sea to the Mediterranean, and from the desert to the river. The Lord grants, but we must possess. The Lord sometimes withholds our blessings until we partner with Him in bold obedience and faith in Him.

This phrase wasn't even the focus in this scripture but as I contemplated the words: "From the desert to the river", I remembered how God promised to meet our every need. I am in a desert right now and need a financial miracle from God just to pay my bills this month. I have been obedient in giving my offerings and recognize this as a tactic of the enemy to discourage me. I have refused to be worried because I can't change my circumstances by worrying. The battle is not mine; it is the Lords. I realize that in a little while I will go from the desert to the river and when I get there, I will pull someone in with me.

A river is defined as a body of water that is constantly moving. It is usually very deep with undercurrents that can sweep you away before you realize it. I am waiting to be swept away by the fast-moving current of the Lord. I have heard that a person can be swept away in an undercurrent in three seconds or less, and since I know that, I am asking the Lord to sweep me away from my problems like a fast-moving undercurrent. I am awaiting my swift change. I know that to Him: "this is but a light thing in HIS sight"

In the desert there is death. There are buzzards and predators. In the desert there are dry dead bones. In the desert is where I was. In the river is where I am going! In the river there is life. In the river there is rebirth. In the river things are being constantly renewed. I'm no longer in the desert! I am now flowing down a swift moving current in the river of abundance. I am flooded with purpose, praise and passion.

My financial situation is changing. I have totally surrendered my life to the Lord. It is in His capable hands that my financial future rests. I have no reason to worry. He said in His word that cattle on a thousand hills belongs to Him. How can I be worried about anything when the creator of the universe is in control of my life? God has given me His gift of the Holy Spirit to live within me.

I can't tell you how long it took for me to realize I was in a current, because things happened very quickly. When I did finally realize I was in the current, I immediately started looking for anyone I knew, that was in a desert. I ministered and taught them how to manage their finances and to seek God in all His wisdom for their lives, in every aspect. And now I'm not the only one that's being blessed by His fast-moving current. I'm pulling as many as I can in the current with me.

No weapon formed against me shall prosper. Take time to pray that God will move in the lives connected to you and that they will be swept away by his love. They shall be swept away by His love and promised rewards.

It's All Good

Psalm 44:8 "In God we boast all day long."

1 Samuel 2:30 "Those who honor me, I will honor."

Jude 1:23 "Save some by snatching them from the fire."

We are His hands and His feet. We need to do what Jesus and the disciples did when they were here. They sought out the hurting, the lost, the poor and the backslidden. In other words, they looked for needy people, and ministered to their needs.

I have good news, and bad news for you. The Lord is pleased with what you are doing but He wants you to know, it's not enough. It's not enough to feed them at Thanksgiving and Christmas. It's not enough to provide a food and clothing pantry if we don't witness to them while they are in our presence.

I wish it was enough to say to the cashier, God bless you. Unfortunately, that is not a call to salvation. We witness and encourage other people, but we only do it sometimes. We do it if they are bleeding, spiritually. We do it if someone is watching us, closely. We do it for at least one person, annually. We do it if they look clean, possibly We do it if they're the same color as we are, maybe.

We do it if we may never see them again, probably. And if we don't do it at all, we say, "they know that I'm a Christian." But how do they know? The Lord says I see all you do and know your thoughts afar off. You are doing some good, but don't boast, because what you are doing is not enough. Don't boast in what you do, boast in the fact that you know God, and you're willing to share His love, with them.

But how will they know? All of us have been saved from something. Tell someone your story. The reason you went through it was because you were destined to be in someone's presence, at some point in your life, that needed to hear your testimony. It made you stronger. It made you a witness of who Jesus is and what He can do for them.

We all get caught up in our own lives. We have family issues. Work issues. Children issues. Marital issues. Relationship issues. We are so focused on ourselves that we don't see anyone else. The Lord said, "He honors those that honor Him." Honor Him by sharing your testimony with others.

Your children and your family members are counting on you. So next time the Holy Spirit whispers in your ear to tell someone about your God. Be bold. Be courageous. Be transparent. Pull someone out of the fire. They need you!

It's all good, but it's not enough.

My Sisters Are Falling

Psalms 94:18 "When I said, my foot slipped: thy mercy held me up O Lord."

Jeremiah 29:13 "You shall seek me and find me, when ye shall search for me with all your heart."

1 John 5:14-15 "He said if we believe and pray according to His will, He will hear us, and when He hears us, He will give us the petitions of our hearts."

The Holy Spirit gave me a message to share with my sisters because so many of them are falling. It seems that in the last days, which we are in now, more and more people are falling away. It seems that as times get harder, we aren't running to God, we are running from God. "The Lord says if you seek me, you will find me." Women used to fill the pews. When husbands, sons, uncles and brothers and fathers stopped coming, or never started, the women still came. But now even the women are falling away.

My Sisters are falling for several reasons. Some are falling because they are tired of being broke, sick and alone. They are the women were determined to be a Proverbs 31 woman. They are the women that raised their children by themselves, worked two jobs, and took care of their household. My sisters are those that were raised in the church, whose mothers taught them to be ladies, not just women. My sisters are those that made a career for themselves even though their parents never graduated high school. My sisters are those that endured racial slurs and sexist comments by co-workers. My sisters are those that fix their own cars, change their own tires, play basketball with their boys, cut their own grass, shovel their own snow, and pay all their own bills. My sisters deal with the telemarketers, sit up all night with sick kids, and then babysit their sisters kids the next morning. My sisters are those that know how to make a meal from scratch, spend fifty dollars on groceries and make them last a month. My sisters are those that live with a man that doesn't respect them or her children. My sisters all called names by the men who claim to love them.

My sisters have kids that are poor, but they don't even know it. My sisters are those that braid hair on the front porch to make ends meet. My sisters are those that sit on executive boards and work in their communities. Some of my sisters have degrees but no self-worth. Some of my sisters are abused and are abusers themselves. I need to help my sisters.

My sisters are many. They are thin, meaty, tall, short, blonde, red haired, tattooed and pierced up. They are all colors. They are single, married or divorced. They are young and they are old. They are employed, unemployed, retired, homemakers, grandmothers, mothers, sisters, best friends, neighbors, nieces and co-workers. They are you and they are me. Most of my sisters are strong and courageous, but some have low self-esteem. some have been emotionally beat down. Some allow it. Some expect it. Some don't report it. Some are full of shame; some are guilty as charged, when it comes to blaming themselves. These are the sisters I am referring to when I say MY SISTERS are Falling.

Are we as women of God not seeking the face of God daily? Are we not committing our bodies as living sacrifices? Have we not become God chasers, but chasers after men, careers, money and vanity? Why are my sisters falling? God has promised to hear us.

What Are My Sisters Falling Into?

My sisters are falling into depression, helplessness, hopelessness, same sex relationships and suicidal ideations. They are falling into the hands of the wrong men. They are falling for fast-talking good-looking men, and men that don't believe in the true and risen Savior. Some are falling for men at the church but not in the church. They are falling, and they are falling quickly. They are not being watchful and prayerful. They are falling and landing on their backs or on their knees- and not in prayer. They have fallen, and they can't get up. My sisters are becoming desperate, not for God. But for a man. Most of my sisters don't even know they have fallen. Some think they have been blessed by God. Even though the man they asked for is nothing like they said they wanted or has nothing in common with them. My sisters have settled, and they don't even know it.

Some sisters know they have fallen but are willing to take their chances on what they think is true love. That is what we call a piece of a man. But God wants us to be made whole, which means complete. He wants nothing less for us than to have a whole man. He would never give us pieces, so we shouldn't accept pieces.

I can see them falling in the spirit. By the thousands I see them falling. The scripture refers to falling from grace. When you fall you are out of control. It is not a state we want to be in, if we are to be stable and unwavering in all our ways.

Some of my sisters had terribly abusive childhoods that God delivered them from. They were abused by fathers, stepfathers, uncles, coaches, cousins, brothers and others. And although they were delivered from their past, they grew up and couldn't wait on who God had for them. Some of them were battered in their previous marriages and made it out with just a few broken bones that eventually healed on their own. But the Lord had promised to make their latter years better than their former years. But they couldn't wait. Isaiah 40:3 says those that wait on the Lord shall renew their strength and so because they didn't wait, they fell.

My Sisters Are Falling

My sisters are giving themselves to men that don't deserve them. Some of my sisters are becoming alcoholics, and drug abusers. Some are climbing the corporate ladder, by any means necessary. Some are consumed with beauty and their physical appearance. Some are turning to other women and getting involved in homosexual relationships. They so desire to please the flesh and belong to someone, that they have crossed the line. They have developed the spirit of Sodom and Gomorrah.

My sisters are falling. Some of my sisters are falling away from God for reasons that have nothing to do with a man. Some are falling because they are tired of being broke. They become workaholics. Some are falling because they are so addicted to T.V that the prayer life they used to have has taken a back seat to shows that open their minds to fake husbands, lovers, and empty relationships.

Some are falling because they come to church out of habit. They don't come to get anything, and they sure don't come to give anything. So, because you reap what you so, they come one way and leave the same way. Then they say – nothing happens at church. You must make things happen! The Bible says Greater works shall we do. What are the greater works? Putting five extra dollars in the offering pan?

My seasoned sisters no longer speak of healing and power. "But you shall receive power after the Holy Spirit has come upon you. I am He that heals thee." My little sisters no longer believe the creator of the universe is aware of their every move. The eyes of the Lord are in every place beholding the evil and the good. They want to look like Beyoncé and sing like Queen Naija- "Away From You" because God is who they're moving further away from. Some of your loved ones will never see you again. Adolescents are giving their virtue to boys for toys.

My sisters are falling. Some are tired of being alone. Some have grown children now and think they should have arrived. Some have said to themselves; "If I don't get married now, I won't ever get married". Some feel old and tired. Some feel frustrated. Some feel wasted. Some feel worthless. Some feel hopeless. Some feel used up. Some feel dried up. Some feel like they are just existing. Some feel unworthy. Some feel life has no meaning. Some feel desperate. Some feel heavy. Some feel depressed. Some feel suicidal. Some just don't feel.

Here are ways to protect yourself from falling. I won't get on a skateboard. Somethings I know will cause me to fall, so I don't do them. It is the same in our natural lives. We know what will cause us to fall. Don't watch that movie, don't go out with those relatives or friends. It's a distraction from the enemy Don't listen to that music. Don't call him back. The Lord always prepares a way of escape. Don't get involved with them if they are not saved. Don't talk to them on the phone, don't go out with them – don't kiss them. If they say, "you think you're too good for me- you can say to yourself, Thou thinkest right! You are a peculiar person. What fellowship has darkness with light? None.

So, what am I supposed to do? How am I supposed to feel like I am worth something? What could make me feel like I am still valuable, attractive, desirable? They that sow in tears shall reap in joy (Psalms126:5). Become more favor minded. No good thing does he withhold from those whose walk is blameless (Psalm 84:11). Begin declaring that you have the favor of God surrounding you. This will bring you to a place of peace, hope and victory like you have never experienced before.

Declare a blessing over your life. Stand in the mirror every morning and declare I am …the head and not the tail, I have supernatural wisdom and receive clear direction for my life. I am blessed with creativity, courage, talent and abundance. I am blessed with strong will self-control and discipline. Now declare that today and every day.

Know Who God is, So You Will Know Who You Are
You have got to remember that you are a child of the Living God! You are who God says you are. A chosen vessel, a royal priesthood, a city set on a hill, an heir of the throne, the apple of His eye, a river in the desert, the salt of the earth, a friend of God. A Proverbs 31 woman.

In the Morning
Wake up every morning and before you open your eyes whisper: Good Morning God of the Universe. Thank you for encamping angels all around me while I slept. Thank you for taking care of my family and loved ones all night long. Thank you for covering me with your blood and allowing me to see another day. Thank you for renewed compassion.

On Your Lunch Break
Have lunch with Him in your office, your car, your house or at McDonalds. Read His word – sit there and pray and let the Holy Spirit build you up. Give Him some Glory.

At the End of Your Workday
Run in your house at the end of the day with expectancy and scream, no weapon formed against me prospered today! He's been waiting all day for you. Sit at your table and eat dinner and tell Him

about your day. I say things like: I felt your presence as I drove to work. I saw you in the eyes of a child I treated today. I felt peace walking with me to my car when I was alone in the parking garage. I felt your presence in the breeze and saw your majesty in the flowers. The sun that you allowed to shine on me reminded me how much you love me. The birds that I saw sitting on the wire took me back to Matthew when you said" not one sparrow falls to the ground without you knowing about it. Know who God is. So, you will know who you are. If you know how much He loves you, you won't fall. Thank you for being my constant someone Lord.

Sisters, listen carefully to wisdom. Be careful of other sisters. Have someone that can intercede with you. Someone that will hold you up when you are falling. Someone that will pray with and for you. Your sisters are not always on the same page as you. How do you know this? They brought you brownies when your husband left, you lost your job, or your daughter got pregnant at 15 years old. If they were on the same page as you, they would have brought you some healing oil. They would have known that you were fasting and seeking God so you wouldn't lose your mind. They would have known that your appetite was not for natural food. They would have known that you were desperate for a word from God.

Stand for what's right. And after you've done all to stand – **Keep on standing! Ask someone to help you stand! Call somebody and tell them you are about to fall! "my foot almost slipped god, but you held me up" but don't give up! Because you will reap if you don't faint –which means you will get what you want if you don't fall!**

Be blessed my sisters!

Every Time I Think of You

Jeremiah 29: 11 "I know the thoughts I think towards you."

Psalm 42:1 "As the deer pants for the water, so my soul pants for You."

Deuteronomy 31:8 "The Lord himself goes before me and with me."

"For I know the plans I have for you...plans to prosper you and give you hope and a future." Variations of this scripture are quoted according to the version of the Bible that you are reading. I have read versions written, that say "I know the plans I have for you. Or "I know the thoughts I have for you, and even- I know the thoughts I think toward you."

When I think about what this scripture means to me, I am reminded of being in love. I remembered how it was whenever I thought about the person I was in love with. My heart was full of anticipation every time I thought of being with them, and spending time talking to them, if only on the phone. Then I thought about how the Lord loves us and how he wants only the best for us. I thought on how only He knows the plans He has for us. He has created us for a purpose, and He is the only one that knows exactly what His plan and purpose is. Because I know the Lord loves me, when I ponder my interpretation of this scripture, this is what it says to me: "I know how I feel whenever I think of You, and whenever I am in Your presence". He loves me more than anyone ever has, or ever will. I know the Lord loves me and I love Him.

Because I know how I feel every time I think of Him, and He feels the same way about me but not in human terms. I know He loves me in a way that no mortal can even explain. When He smiles at me – my heart smiles back at Him. When He blesses me with compassion, courage, a spirit of forgiveness and a heart full of praise, I am moved to tears. These attributes come only through constant communication with the Holy Spirit, prayer and fasting.

I know He is watching me and holding me close to Him. I know He is protecting me from danger that I don't even see. I know He is pouring out His daily blessings on me.

I thank the Lord for birds, flowers and trees. For laughter, for pain, for sunshine, for rain. For the great white shark to the tiniest ant. The Lord knows that I appreciate Him allowing me to hear the birds singing in the morning. Whenever I see the flowers pushing their way through the soil in the spring, or view apple orchards, corn fields and mountains my heart melts. I thank Him For insight and wisdom. For a spirit that pants after You and your presence like the deer pants after the water brooks. How awesome you are mighty God, for all you have done, I give you praise. You alone are worthy. God wants us to feel excited about spending time in His presence every day. He is waiting for us to want to spend time with Him.

I think of my Lord as always being with me, because He said He goes with me and before me in all circumstances. I know His Holy spirit is in my home when I'm not. I know His spirit is in my car when I'm driving. I know He's gone before me when I don't see danger ahead. I know, that He knows all, and sees all, even before it happens.

I think of Him awaiting my arrival when I get off work. I imagine Him standing at the door and saying: I've been waiting all day to commune with you. And I am anticipating spending time in His presence. I have been filled with a spirit of praise all day, and thoughts of peace and joy have consumed me. So now when I get home, because I live alone. I open my door, put down my purse and say as loud as I can. Honey I'm home! I am as glad to be in The Lords presence, as He is to have me in His presence. I delight in Him, the way He delights in me.

Retrain Yourself

1 Peter 5:8 "Be sober and watch, for your adversary walks about like a roaring lion, seeking whom he may devour."

Mark 10:8 "Behold, we have left everything and followed you Lord.'

The Lord has it all, is all, and wants the best for us. Unfortunately, we don't have that, or believe that for several reasons. The main reason is that we believe the lies of the enemy instead of Gods truth in His word. We should not give the enemy any credit, because the world already gives him enough. We often hear Christians saying things like "the enemy is good at his job" or "Satan never gets tired" or "he's diligent in hunting us down and making our lives miserable." Stop giving him all that credit. One scripture that I hear Christians quote more often than the Lord's Prayer is " Satan is seeking who he can devour like a lion seek his prey." Unfortunately we all know that scripture all too well.

The world already gives Satan enough credit. He is empowered when he hears Christians voicing how strong and relentless he is. Those comments don't offend him. He's glad you're spending that much time thinking about him. He's not mad about it, he's glad about it! That conversation should never take place from any Christian. Hollywood says it like this "no ink, is bad ink." It simply means that as long as you're writing about them, they are at least being acknowledged. Good or bad, their name is seen by thousands, in print.

Retrain your thoughts. Think about the true living God. Practice saying this: I will not spend my time edifying anyone other than you Lord. I will speak positive affirmations about You Lord, and give You alone all praise. I surrender my thoughts to you, I surrender my words to you and I surrender my will to you and only You.

No More Towels

Exodus14:13 "Don't be afraid. Stand firm and see the salvation of the Lord."

1 Corinthians 16:9 "For a great door has been opened for me."

Proverbs 4:25 "Fix your gaze directly before you."

Resignation not accepted in the workplace is what we say. In the spirit what God says is I'm not accepting any more towels to be thrown in. If I didn't you can't! God is tired of us getting to the point where we keep saying we are going to throw in the towel. We get to the point that we get tired of preaching to empty pews. Singing to the faithful few. Inviting members to their own church. Witnessing to those that are supposed to be saved. Telling them not to give up. Hang on. It's almost over. You can do it! Don't give up.

If Job didn't. If Paul didn't. If Gideon didn't. If Moses didn't. If Elisha, and Elijah didn't. If the disciples didn't… They suffered more tragedy and trials than we can even imagine and yet they didn't quit. If Jesus Himself didn't, what makes you think you can give up. The battle is not yours it's the Lords! Things aren't going to get easier, so you need to make up your minds now that you are going to remain strong and faithful. If you can't stand being talked about, lied on and broke all at the same time, you are not going to be able to stand against the enemy in the end time, which you are already in. Don't give up now. It's almost over.

He is saying that if He didn't throw in the towel what makes you think you can. He isn't accepting any more towels. He didn't say well I am tired of them seeing me work miracles and not believing me. He didn't say, I am not going to raise anyone else from the dead, heal anyone else from leprosy, restore anyone else's sight. People still don't believe that I am the son of God.

What if Jesus said, I am throwing in the towel. I give up. I can't do it any more God! I give in. But He didn't throw in the towel when He was betrayed by Judas. He didn't tell God; I am not going to the cross for them. They chose Barabbas over me. I am not going to be beat for these ungrateful people. That's where I draw the line Lord. He didn't even throw in the towel when they mocked Him, spit on them, put a crown of thorns on His head and exposed His nakedness. Then nailed His hands and feet to the cross.

We are to represent Jesus here on the earth, so if He didn't quit, we can't either. What is so hard now that is making you want to throw in the towel? You will constantly have something, Finances or the lack thereof? Raising those kids by yourself? I know what it is for the single women and some men. It is not having a warm body to snuggle with, so I am throwing in the towel. So now it's thrown in, so now you have someone. So now it's something else. So now what? So now you're having problems on your job.

It's always going to be something that will make you want to throw in the towel. It is supposed to always be something. If you are not being challenged to pray, challenged to change, challenged to do better, challenged as the Lord was, you won't get stronger and you won't grow. The Lord says there will always be something. Enemy if necessary. I am not throwing in the towel. And you shouldn't either. but just remember I am your constant someone.

God is tired of hearing those of you that are His, saying you are even thinking about throwing in the towel. We Shouldn't insult Him like that. We all have issues. Young people – you are here because your mama and daddy didn't throw in the towel. Your mamas are here because their mamas didn't throw in the towel. We are all here because Jesus – didn't throw in the towel!

I challenge you to change. I challenge you to keep going! I challenge you to live!

Always Yes

Deuteronomy 31:8 "The Lord himself goes before you and with you."

Isaiah 41:10 "I will uphold you with my righteous right hand."

Hebrews 13:5 "I will never leave or forsake you."

I can remember being in church for over two years having to fight a battle and consequently the war that the enemy had waged against me. I can remember him trying his best to get me to do and say things that were out of character for me and would've been displeasing to the Lord. He was trying to take me down. His plan was to get me to be so oppositional, so negative that I would not be an effective Christian and certainly not an effective warrior.

I can remember having thoughts come into my mind, and thinking to myself, that's not how I feel at all. I remember apologizing to the pastor one day for being disagreeable. Her response was, "I didn't know you were being disagreeable." I wasn't trying to be disagreeable. I was trying not to be, but the enemy was trying to get me to cause dissension. It didn't work. I can vividly remember, sitting right there on the front pew binding ungodly spirits and pressing through as hard as I could because the Lord had let me know that the devils plan was to take me out by any means necessary. I can remember saying "who used to sit here?" But I didn't change my seat because whoever would have sat there, instead of me, may not have been able to press through and bind those spirits.

I cried out one day to the Lord: hallelujah, praise Your name, You alone are worthy. But it seemed that I couldn't break the bonds that were not allowing me to break through. I remember saying: Thank you, touch me, forgive me, I repent. Still not getting what I am looking for. Lord what is it, I'm not giving up, but I am getting tired. I then said to the Lord, Ok God: "I surrender" Help! Help! Help! But that wasn't it either. Then His spirit spoke to my spirit and made it very clear. "All I want you to say is- YES!!!

That's all! Quit trying to make it so complicated. Just tell me yes. I have things for you to do. Places for you to go. People for you to talk to. Just tell me yes. I appreciate your praise, but I need to know that you will go where I say, do what I tell you, not go where I tell you, and worship and praise me. You may have to get up at three in the morning and get on your knees. You may have to give a little more than you're giving. You may have to stay up late and get up early. You may have to pray alone for a while longer. You may have to stand alone in your beliefs, but if you stay focused and stay in the word, I will always hold you up. You may stay single until I send someone. You may have to learn to smile when you want to cry. You may have to do without, so someone else wont. You may have to stand alone, but if you are willing to tell Me YES, I will never leave you or forsake you.

You God Are The One

Genesis 1-2 "In the beginning God created the heavens and the earth."

Matthew 10:29 "Not a single sparrow will fall to the ground without God knowing it."

Ecclesiastics 3:11 "He has made everything beautiful in His own time."

Job 38 1-4 "Where were you when I laid the earths foundation."

The creator of the universe

The creator of everyday, past, present and future

The one who said "Let there be light, and there was light" but the sun wasn't created until the fourth day

The one who created male and female

The one who gave His only begotten son

The lifter up of bowed down heads

The one who spoke, and everything came into being

The one who parted the red sea

The one who makes rivers in deserts

The one who raised the dead

The one whose compassions are new every morning

The one that holds me in the middle of the night

The one that takes care of the sparrows

The one that put each star in the sky

The catcher of fallen stars

The one that uplifts, sets free, and delivers

The one that gives me reason to get out of bed

The one who heals

The one that called Gideon mighty

The one that delivered Daniel from the lions

The one that changed Saul to Paul

The one that woke me up this morning

The one that appeared in the fiery furnace

The one that caused the sun to shine

The one that kept me safe all night

The one that raised Lazarus from the dead

The forgiver of all sin

The one who is the way when there is no way

The one who is the air I breathe

The one that keeps me from falling

The promise maker and the promise keeper

The author of peace

The one who keeps me from worry

The one who made every snowflake different

The one who made the flea and the elephant

The one who created lightening and speaks through thunder

The one who causes the wind to blow and the seas not to overflow

The one who created DNA

The one who made every man to have his own set of fingerprints

The giver of peace

The one who loves me more than I love myself

The one who created water to fall from the sky

The one who created oxygen

The one who created the solar system and holds every planet in place

The one who created light and light came at 186,000 miles per second. And is still coming

The giver of every good and perfect gift

The one who created laughter

The one who gives us ideas to get wealth

The one who reminds me that I am a good mother

The one who held me together when I was falling apart

The one who created the sunrise with me in mind

The one who said, don't take your own life, I can fix it

The one who created life

The one who created death

The one who created emotions

The one who created touch

The one who reminds me of His covenant with the rainbow

The one who created pansies, lilies, roses, and wildflowers, but also created thorns, cactuses, weeds

The one who created oceans and tornadoes, earthquakes, waterfalls, mountains, valleys and meadows

The one who changes hearts

The only one that is worthy of all praise

The one that saved me from my sins

The one that's waiting for me to live eternally with Him when I leave this earth

The one that said I will never leave you

The one that said I LOVE YOU!

The One God - My everything

I Forgive Me

Ephesians 4:32 "Be kind and compassionate to one another."

Luke 6:37 "Do not judge and you will not be judged."

2 Corinthians 5:17 "If anyone is in Christ he is a new creation."

Sometimes what happens when we are kids is that we are in a dispute with another child, and our parents tell us to go and apologize. We never want to do it, but we know that we must, or we will face the consequences from our parents. What has usually transpired is something that we didn't even mean to do. We got caught up in the moment and said, or did something that hurt someone, and forgot that words can't be taken back, once they are spoken.

What happens a lot of times in our spiritual lives, is that whatever we have done, whether it be hurting someone's feelings, experimenting with drugs, having an abortion, stealing, cheating, lying on our taxes, spreading gossip, or any other skeletons in our closet. What we must realize is that when we gave our life to Him, all was forgiven. We don't know what it is that is holding us back in our relationship with the Lord. We feel distanced from Him when we harbor unforgiveness.

We can't forgive ourselves for the way our kids turned out. We replay it over and over in our minds. If I had just done things differently. We can't forgive ourselves for not being more aggressive in our jobs or handling our finances differently. We can't forgive ourselves for all the people we have hurt as we progressed through life. We can't forget those that have died that we didn't get a chance to make it right with. The Lord has also forgiven us. The most crucial piece in this dilemma, is unforgiveness to ourselves. If we would just stand in the mirror and ask the Lords forgiveness of what we have done, and then actually forgive ourselves we could go on with our lives. Forgiving ourselves is harder to do than to ask someone else to forgive us. But the Lord wants us to forget it. He said: "Any man that is in Christ is a new creature All things have passed away, and look, everything is now new." There is nothing we can do that would make Him not love us. His word says He has cast our sins into the sea of forgetfulness. Our past sins are totally gone. God's love is unconditional. I forgive me Lord.

Take a few moments and list all the things you need to forgive yourself for, and let it go!

_____

_____

_____

_____

_____

_____

_____

_____

_____

_____

_____

_____

_____

_____

_____

_____

_____

_____

_____

_____

_____

_____

ABOUT THE AUTHOR

Shantelle Hawkins is married to Saxophone Recording artist Pastor Terence Hawkins, together they have four wonderful children. Shantelle has laid and travailed on the altar for over (30) years to birth her ministry. It was the mighty hands of God that anointed her vocals and qualified her to produce an authentic sound that shifts and shakes the atmosphere.

Shantelle has faced many trials, and has now written the warriors manual as a result of her recent fight and victory over breast cancer. Shantelle knows that God gave her the strength to fight and win, and shares her story and information on spiritual warfare and how to defeat the enemy through the power of prayer, praise, intercession and worship.

Shantelle was given the name "Fearless Prophetic Worshipper," because her prophetic praise echoes deliverance as she bravely goes to war against the powers of darkness and often hear the "Sounds of Victory".

Mrs. Hawkins has travelled from State to State sharing the platforms and pulpits with many of gospel greats. She describes her most valued and memorable moments being the time spent pursuing the presence of the Holy Spirit, witnessing the atmosphere shifting and yokes being broken off of God's people through worship.

Shantelle is employed with the State of Michigan and is a graduate of Michigan State University, where she received her Bachelor's Degree in Criminal Justice. She obtained her Master's in Business Administration (M.B.A) from Spring Arbor University.

Shantelle is a faithful minister at Mt. Zion Church of Deliverance where she serves alongside her husband, Pastor Terence as the Praise and Worship Leader and leader of the women's ministry. She has a heart for hurting women, abused children and a passion for souls. She is the Founder/Executive Director of Daughters or Promise which is a faith based teen pregnancy prevention and self- esteem non-profit organization for adolescent girls in Michigan.

Shantelle truly believes that Praise is our weapon and rejoices in knowing that we serve an awesome God who is able to do exceedingly and abundantly far above all we could ever ask or think. She is a living witness that God is a healer!

ABOUT THE AUTHOR

Wisdom is defined as the ability to make good decisions based on experience and knowledge.

I am now in a place where I am able to help others with real life issues based on the wisdom the Lord has blessed me with. I have been in many situations that were challenging, physically , emotionally and spiritually. I was once in a dark place, but the darkness didn't consume me. It only made me appreciate the Son, more.

I am grateful for my mother who led me to the Lord. My daughter and best friend, who I gave birth to. My only son is a blessing in ways he's not even aware of. I'm grateful for my younger sister who shared her platform with me and my older sister who has always been my personal cheerleader. I am now married to the most amazing man I have ever met. I would never have imagined that I would be blessed with such a loving, caring and devoted man of God.

I was destined to be an encourager, a bridge and a strong tower. I recognize my blessings and appreciate Gods favor. I'm growing in the grace and favor of the Lord, and will continue encouraging others to do the same until He comes back.

Charisse Chatman

Made in the USA
Lexington, KY
30 October 2019